Violent Dances Fade · CHOREAE VIOLENTAE DISSOLVVNTVR
Libertarian Poetical Fragments

AD VITAM REDITVS

A Collection of fifty-one Latin Epigrams by
Stefano Losi

And their English and Italian translations

With three Elegies by Marco Mathieu

MMDCCLXXIIII aVc

Violent Dances Fade · CHOREAE VIOLENTAE DISSOLVVNTVR
Libertarian Poetical Fragments

A multimedia art and poetry project of
Stefano Losi

Perpetvae Memoriae

Fratris Mei
DCLXVII – DCXCIX aVc

Patris Mei
MMDCXCV – MMDCCLXV aVc

New York – Milan – London
www.ViolentDancesFade.com
editor@violentdancesfade.com

ISBN: 978-1-7352816-0-5

"Timeless · On the contrary, inside time · And beyond
Significant · Blunt · Stirring, most of all"
Marco MATHIEU
Writer and Journalist · La Repubblica, Rome

"Most impressive work · A scholarly writer"
Steve AOKI
Composer and Musician · Los Angeles

"A splendid union · Poetry as universal value"
Antonio Maria COSTA
Under-Secretary-General · United Nations

"Stefano seizes the gold that the moment presents"
Renato MIRACCO
Art Critic and Historian · Washington DC

"In a world that has decided to go faster Stefano with his art and poetry has decided
to go deeper in our soul"
Paolo GALLO
Writer and Professor · Geneva

"A very physical art · Raw material · And most importantly, alive"
Roberto FARANO
Composer and Musician · Turin

"Stefano moves me with his words, forms and vision
almost as much as he inspires me with his thirst for life"
Jonny HETHERINGTON
Composer and Musician · Vancouver

"Rich of sensuality and sensibility, the lines provide colour to the eyes"
Samira LEGLIB
Journalist · La Repubblica, New York

"One of the rare artists who can negotiate seemingly opposing disciplines
with rigor, and unite them in one cathartic gesture"
Chambliss GIOBBI
Artist, Actor and Composer · New York

3

*"CUI DONO LEPIDVM NOVVM LIBELLVM
ARIDA MODO PVMICE EXPOLITVM?"*

On the front cover: PHOEBVS (detail)
Brushed Steel and Cast Crystal (17"x10"x10" · 43x25x25cm)

Table of contents · Indice

"PLVS VNO MANEAT PERENNE SAECLO"

Indice

Pagina

Biografia *14*

Prefazione *18*

Epigrammi ed Elegie *23*

Cyclvs materiei   *25*
I · Motvs   *28*
II · Velvm   *32*
III · Aditvs   *36*
IV · Prooemivm   *40*
Sopore   *50*
Canto dell'amato   *54*
Carme LI   *58*
Carme CI   *62*
Spore   *66*
Rifrazioni   *70*
Solitudine   *74*
Umidore   *78*
Poeta   *82*
Efebo decaduto   *88*
Iridi   *94*
Kouros   *98*
Persona   *102*
Demone   *106*
M M XVIII   *110*
Fremito blu   *114*
Filigrame   *118*
Fiume   *128*
Tuffatori di anime   *132*
Io   *136*

Pagina

Poesia	140
Padre	144
Kore	148
Febbre crepuscolare	154
Rinascita	160
Umo e luce	172
Impressione	178
Illusione	182
Aranceto odoroso	186
Cartagine	190
Noi	194
Oceano	198
Frammento CLXVIII	202
Mandorla	206
Ozio inquieto	210
Sindone	214
Shulammite	220
Sacerdotessa	228
Furore febeo	234
Ponente lacedemone	244
Talamo	250
Berlino	256
Corruzione empirea	238
Lene fremore	264
Iride viridea	270
Ebrieta'	276
Reazione	280

Table of contents

Page

Biography *15*

Preface *20*

Elegies and Epigrams *23*

Cyclvs materiei   *25*
I · Vibration   *26*
II · Veil   *30*
III · Opening   *34*
IV · Prelude   *38*
Drowsiness   *48*
Beloved's lyric   *52*
Poem LI   *56*
Poem CI   *60*
Spores   *64*
Refractions   *68*
Solitude   *72*
Dampness   *76*
Poet   *80*
Fallen ephebos   *84*
Irides   *92*
Kouros   *96*
Persona   *100*
Demon   *104*
M M XVIII   *108*
Blue tremble   *112*
Filigrees   *116*
River   *126*
Divers of souls   *130*
I   *134*

Page

Poetry	*138*
Father	*142*
Kore	*146*
Crepuscular fever	*150*
Rebirth	*158*
Humus and light	*168*
Impression	*176*
Illusion	*180*
Fragrant orange grove	*184*
Carthago	*188*
We	*192*
Ocean	*196*
Fragment CLXVIII	*200*
Almond	*204*
Unquiet idleness	*208*
Shroud	*212*
Shulammite	*216*
Priestess	*224*
Phebean wrath	*232*
Occidental lands of Lacedaemon	*242*
Thalamus	*246*
Berlin	*254*
Transcendent corruption	*258*
Subtle tremble	*262*
Green iris	*266*
Inebriety	*274*
Reaction	*278*

Violent Dances Fade · CHOREAE VIOLENTAE DISSOLVVNTVR
Libertarian Poetical Fragments

Biography · Biografia

PERTVRBATIONE ANIMI GIGNOR
NON INTERMISSO MOTV PONTI METHYMNAE

Biografia

SONO GENERATO DALL'INQUIETUDINE
Il movimento ininterrotto dei mari di Metimna

STEFANO LOSI è nato nel 1969 sul lago di Como, vicino a Milano, dove ha ricevuto un'educazione classica in letteratura ed arti visive. Dopo la laurea all'Università Luigi Bocconi di Milano del 1993, ha ricoperto posizioni manageriali in diverse istituzioni internazionali, ed è ora ufficiale senior dell'Organizzazione delle Nazioni Unite a New York, dove è anche Presidente del Circolo Culturale Letterario. Nel 2005 è stato nominato *Cavaliere della Repubblica Italiana* dal Presidente Ciampi.

"Violent Dances Fade · Choreae Violentae Dissolvvntvr" è il suo progetto di arti multimediali e poesia, creato a Milano nel 1991, e poi sviluppato a Londra e New York. "Choreae Violentae Dissolvvntvr" combina sculture in bronzo, acciaio, vetro e luci LED, musica contemporanea e spoken word, e studi su lino della figura umana in olii e minerali ossidati, con una poesia epigrammatica Latina. Dopo una lunga serie di eventi organizzati fino dai primi anni '90 in Europa, che hanno incluso mostre e letture di poesia in spazi sia formali che alternativi, da gallerie a unioni di lavoratori e centri sociali, la sua arte ha ricevuto l'onore di diverse mostre personali alle Nazioni Unite ed in affermate gallerie di New York. La sua poesia e' apparsa in antologie letterarie internazionali, quali Retina Literary Journal. Antonio Maria Costa, Sotto Segretario-Generale delle Nazioni Unite, ha scritto: *"È questo un connubio splendido. C'è nelle parole di queste poesie la stessa speranza che nutro quando osservo il mondo."*

Cinque volumi di arte e poesia sono stai pubblicati nel 1996, 2001, 2010, 2013 e 2016, fornendo una prospettiva del lavoro dell'autore nei rispettivi periodi creativi. L'arte di Stefano Losi è stata parte di diverse pubblicazioni internazionali, tra cui un volume su artisti contemporanei italiani curato da Renato Miracco, e pubblicato sotto gli auspici del Ministero degli Affari Esteri.
L'autore continua a creare arti visive e poesia a Chelsea, New York.

www.ViolentDancesFade.com
editor@violentdancesfade.com

Biography

I AM GENERATED BY RESTLESSNESS
The uninterrupted movement of the seas of Methymna

STEFANO LOSI was born in 1969 in Lake Como, near Milan, where he was classically educated in literature and fine arts. After his graduate degree at the Luigi Bocconi University of Milan in 1993, he covered senior management roles in different international institutions, and he is currently senior official of the United Nations in New York, where he is also President of the UNSRC Literary Cultural Circle. In 2005 he was nominated *Knight of the Italian Republic* by President Ciampi.

"Violent Dances Fade · Choreae Violentae Dissolvvntvr" is his multimedia art and poetry project created in Milan in 1991, and further developed in London and New York. It combines sculptures in bronze, steel, cast glass and LED lights, contemporary music and spoken word, and linen studies of the human figure in oils and oxidized metal minerals, with an epigrammatic Latin poetry. After a long series of events organized since the early 1990s in Europe, including shows and poetry readings in formal and alternative spaces, ranging from galleries, to workers unions and social centers, his art has been honored with different solo exhibitions at the United Nations and in established galleries in New York. His poetry has been part of international literary antologies, as Retina Literary Journal. Antonio Maria Costa, Under-Secretary-General of the United Nations, wrote: *"This is a splendid union. In the words of these poems I find the same hope I cherish when I observe the world."*

Five books collecting his art and epigrams, providing an overview of the author's work in the respective creative periods, were published in 1996, 2001, 2010, 2013 and 2016. Stefano Losi's work has been featured in different international publications, among which a book on Italian contemporary artists curated by Renato Miracco, and published under the auspices of the Italian Ministry of Foreign Affairs.
The author continues to create art and poetry in Chelsea, New York.

www.ViolentDancesFade.com
editor@violentdancesfade.com

Preface · *PROOEMIVM* · *Prefazione*

Preface

The silent contemplation of unquiet tears
On glass windows of violet and amber
As primordial vibration

Illuminates me

PROOEMIVM

MVTA CONTEMPLATIO INQVIETARVM DACRVMARVM
IN VITRIS VIOLACEIS
VT MOTVS PRIMVS

ME ILLVMINAT

Prefazione

La muta contemplazione di inquiete lacrime
Su vetrate di viola ambrate
Quale vibrazione prima

Mi illumina

Violent Dances Fade · CHOREAE VIOLENTAE DISSOLVVNTVR
Libertarian Poetical Fragments

Elegies · Elegie

CYCLVS MATERIEI

I · MOTVS

I

As a foetus
Weak
Exposed

I am generated by unquietness
The faint vibration
Of the monotony of the white surface of the smooth waters

Unripe thoughts
Of a light veil of frost
Bead pale olive trees of silver

The original dawn

The cold of water
Of the lagoon of light of the vitreous appearance
Dissolves in a shiver
Faint at first
Then more perceivable

In the tepid tremor of the body
Of the instinctive motion

In *effused rain*

Vibration

I

TAMQVAM FETVS
DEBILIS
NVDVS

PERTVRBATIONE ANIMI GIGNOR
MOTV LEVI
CANDIDORVM AEQVORVM SIMILITVDINIS AQVARVM

ACERBAE COGITATIONES
LEVIS VELI PRVINARVM
CLARAS OLIVAS ARGENTEAS MARGARITIS ORNANT

PRIMA LVX INNATA

ALGOR AQVAE
PALVDIS IMAGINE VITREA LVCIS
HORRORE DISSOLVITVR
ANTEA SVBTILI
POSTEA SENSIBILIORE

IN TEPIDIS CORPORIS SALTIBVS
NATVRALI MOTV

EFFVSIS IN IMBRIBVS

MOTVS

I

Come un feto
Debole
Scoperto

Sono generato dall'inquietudine
La lieve vibrazione
Della monotonia della bianca superficie delle acque levigate

I pensieri acerbi
Di un velo leggiero di brina
Imperlano chiari olivi argentei

L'alba originale

Il gelo dell'acqua
Della laguna di luce dall'apparenza vitrea
Si dissolve in un brivido
Prima sottile
Poi piu' sensibile

Nei tepidi sussulti del corpo
dal moto istintivo

In *effuse pioggie*

MOTVS

CYCLVS MATERIEI

II · VELVM

II

As voice of the moist veil
The rain
Incessant water sombre of restlessness
Talks to my eyelashes

Amongst the wind
Faint tremble

With inebriated face I approach my lips to yours
Pale
Damp of fine copper

Your fickle mouth
Soaked of rain
Opens to an acrid contraction

An impure spasm
Uninterrupted

Exquisite violence

The extreme vehemence
Coagulates in shadow the tension of the eyelids

Until the convulsive visage
Dissolves the power
In effused essence

Of *Etruscan brume*

Veil

II

VT VDO VELO VOX
IMBER
ASSIDVA AQVA TRISTIS TREPIDATIONE
CILIA MEA ADLOQVITVR

IN VENTO
TENVI TREMORE

VVLTV EBRIO LABRA MEA TVIS ADMOVEO
PALLIDIS
EX SVBTILI AERE VDIS

OS TVVM VOLVBILE
IMBRE MADEFACTVM
ACRI CONTRACTIONI APERIT

SPASMO CORRVPTO
NVNQVAM INTERMISSO

EXQVISITA VI

VEHEMENTIA EXTREMA
IN VMBRA PALPEBRARVM INTENTIONEM DENSET

DVM CONCITATVS VVLTVS
POTENTIAM DISSOLVIT
IN EFFVSO ODORE

ETRVSCARVM BRVMARVM

VELVM

II

Quale voce dal velo umido
La pioggia
Incessante acqua tetra d'irrequietezza
Parla alle mie ciglia

Fra il vento
Tenue tremore

Con volto ebro accosto le mie labbra alle tue
Esangui
Umide di rame sottile

La tua bocca volubile
Molle di pioggia
Apre ad una contrazione acre

Uno spasimo impuro
Ininterrotto

Squisita violenza

La veemenza estrema
Addensa in ombra la tensione delle palpebre

Finche' il viso convulso
Discioglie la potenza
In effuso effluvio

Di *etrusche brume*

VELVM

CYCLVS MATERIEI

III · ADITVS

III

The violet flat surface
Of waters
Opens to the evening brume

In motionless Etruscan green
Reflects the aridity of rocks livid of ash

Celebrates the inevitable release
Of existence

The breath of the sun stops at the edges of the port
And the Florentine cypresses
Tight in the shade
Permeate the air of aroma of absence

Through the filigree of the hair
The eyes search for an opening
They follow your white flowing tunic

Timidly I touch its pure gauzes of linen
Of the dying scent

Silently you turn
You guide me with your hand
You collect my docile body
Devoid of shadow

Finally myself

My turbid pupils
Reemerge within your ashen glance

In *mute haze*

Opening

III

VIOLACEVM AEQVOR
AQVARVM
BRVMIS VESPERTINIS APERIT

ETRVSCO IN IMMOTO VIRIDI
REPERCVTIT ARIDITATEM RVPIVM CINERE LIVIDARVM

CELEBRAT INEVITABILEM RELICTIONEM
VITAE

AVRA SOLIS CONSISTIT IN PORTVS ORE
ET FLORENTINAE CVPRESSVS
IN VMBRA DENSETAE
AEREM EX ODORE ABSENTIAE PERMEANT

INTER FILORVM GRANVM CAPILLI
OCVLI ADITVM SCRVTANTVR
ASPICIVNT CANDIDAM TVNICAM PROMISSAM

TIMIDE CANDIDA CARBASA SVA ATTINGO
MORIBVNDIS ODORIBVS

TACITE TE VERTIT
ME MANV DVCIS
MEVM CORPVS OBSEQVENS COLLIGIT
VMBRA NVDVM

AD VLTIMVM EGOMET

MEAE PVPILLAE TVRBIDAE EMERGVNT
EX INTERIORE PARTE ASPECTVS TVI CINEREI

IN MVTIS CALIGINIBVS

ADITVS

III

L'equòre violaceo
Delle acque
Apre alle brume della sera

In immobile verde etrusco
Riflette l'aridita' di rocce livide di cenere

Celebra il rilascio inevitabile
Dell'esistenza

L'alito del sole si ferma ai margini del porto
Ed i cipressi fiorentini
Stretti in ombra
Permeano l'aria d'aroma d'assenza

Fra la filigrana dei capelli
Gli occhi cercano un varco
Seguono la tua bianca tunica fluente

Timidamente ne sfioro le garze candide di lino
Dai profumi morenti

In silenzio ti volgi
Mi conduci per mano
Raccogli il mio corpo remissivo
Spoglio d'ombra

Finalmente me stesso

Le mie pupille torbide
Riaffiorano entro il tuo sguardo cinereo

In *mute caligini*

ADITVS

CYCLVS MATERIEI

IV · PROOEMIVM

IV

You forgot me

As a mute shadow
I wander on crepuscular distances
In acrid yearning

I flutter on the reflecting waters

I become the retributive justice
The isolating power
The eternal ire of Nemesis

I taste its sublime violence
In noble solitude

On a bed white of ivory
I observe my remains

From my pyre evaporates myrrh of darkest honey

With arid eyes
I watch my ashes
Returning to the bitter soil

In a light of glass
Prelude

Of *unripe frost*

Prelude

IV

OBLITA MEI ES

VT MVTA VMBRA
VESPERTINAS SVPER LONGINQVITATES VAGOR
IN ACRI ANIMI PERTVRBATIONE

SVPER SPECVLVM AQVARVM VOLITO

SVM IVSTITIA VLTRIX
POTENTIA SECLVDENS
AETERNA IRA NEMESEOS

GVSTO EIVS CLARISSIMAM VIM
IN LIBERALI SOLITVDINE

IN EBVRNEO LECTO
MEMBRA MEA INTVEOR

MYRRHA OBSCVRISSIMO MELLE A PYRA MEA EXHALAT

ARIDIS OCVLIS
CONTEMPLOR CINEREM MEAM
AMARAM IN TERRAM REDEVNTEM

IN VITREA LVCE
PROOEMIO

ACERBARVM PRVINARVM

PROOEMIVM

IV

Mi hai dimenticato

Quale ombra muta
Vago su lontananze crepuscolari
In smania acre

Aleggio sullo specchio delle acque

Divengo la giustizia ultrice
Isolatrice potenza
L'eterna ira di Nemesi

Ne assaporo la sublime violenza
In nobile solitudine

Su un letto bianco d'avorio
Osservo il mio corpo esanime

Dalla mia pira evapora una mirra di miele scurissimo

Con occhi aridi
Assisto alle mie ceneri
Tornare nell'amara terra

In una luce di vetro
Preludio

Di *acerbe brine*

PROOEMI*V*M

CREPVSCVLVM SYCOMORŌRVM (detail)
Steel, Cast Crystal and LED Lights (18"x11"x11" · 45x28x28cm)

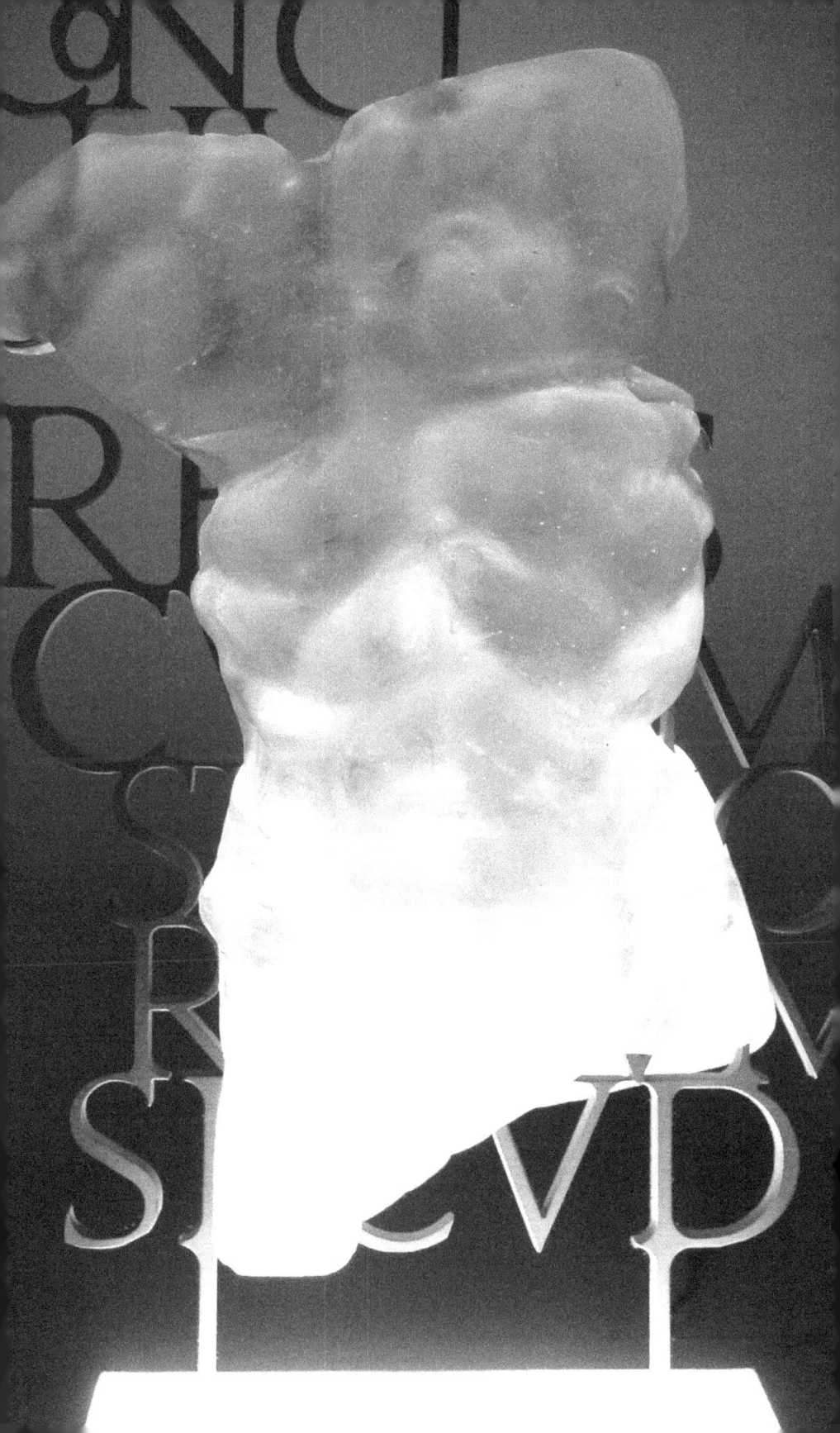

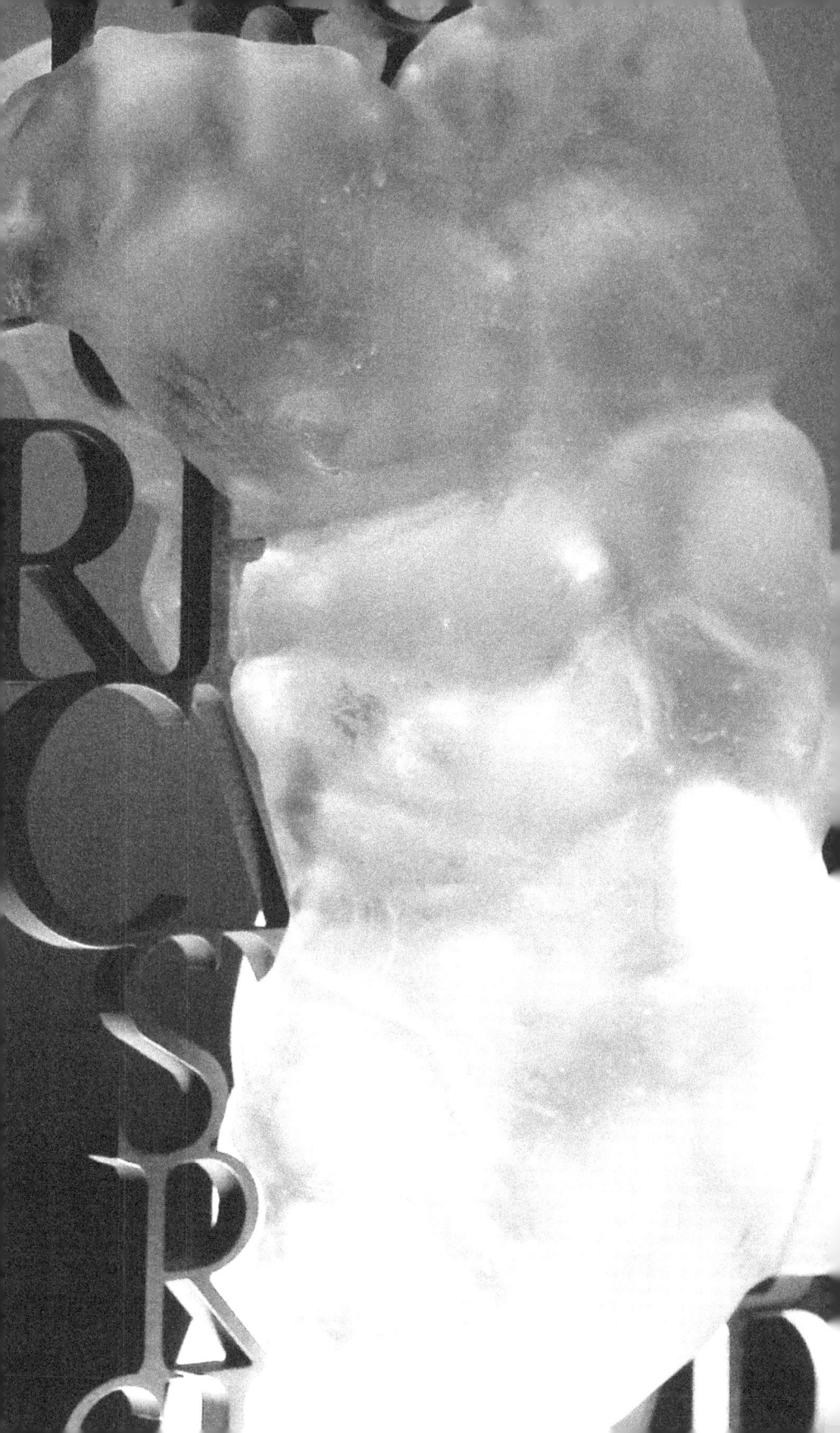

CREPVSCVLVM SYCOMORŌRVM (detail)
Steel, Cast Crystal and LED Lights (18"x11"x11" · 45x28x28cm)

SOPOR

Arabic cassia evaporates
With a delicate gesture you pour most pure nectar

Drowsiness oozes

Drowsiness

CASIA ARABICA VAPORAT
LEVI GESTV EFFVNDIS NECTAR PVRISSIMVM

SOPOR STILLAT

SOPOR

Cassia arabica vapora
Con gesto lieve versi un nettare purissimo

Stilla sopore

Sopore

AMASII CANTVS

Under a sky virgin of clouds
As lacerated veil
I perceive your breath

Last essence

Suffused of opaqueness
Obscurity wraps the earth

In embrace I collect your reclined visage
My beloved

My arid eyes linger
On your eyelids mute of shadow
Profound
Of virile expression

The heroic nudity

The hands lifeless
On golden melilots
Of your gentle blood
Still unquiet

My only bitter words

Do not leave me I pray you
You know how much I love your lyric

Beloved's lyric

SVB INTACTO NVBIBVS CAELO
VT LACERATVM VELVM
SPIRITVM TVVM SENTIO

VLTIMAM VIM

TENEBRAE TERRAS INVOLVVNT
OPACITATE SVFFVSAE

RECLINATVM VVLTVM TVVM IN AMPLEXVM TOLLO
AMASIE MI

OCVLI MEI ARIDI INSISTVNT
IN PALPEBRIS TVIS VMBRA MVTIS
ACVTIS
ORE VIRILI

HEROICO CORPORE NVDO

LENTIS MANIBVS
IN MELILOTIS AVREIS
SANGVINE TVO GENTILI
ADHVC INQVIETO

SOLA ACERBA VERBA MEA

NOLI ME RELINQVERE TE ORO
QVANTVM AMEM CANTVM TVVM SCIS

AMASII CANTVS

Sotto un cielo vergine di nubi
Quale velo lacerato
Avverto il tuo respiro

Ultima essenza

Soffusa d'opacita'
L'oscurita' avvolge la terra

In abbraccio raccolgo il tuo viso reclinato
Mio amato

I miei occhi aridi si fermano
Sulle tue palpebre mute d'ombra
Profonde
Di espressione virile

La nudita' eroica

Le mani inerti
Su meliloti dorati
Del tuo sangue gentile
Ancora irrequieto

Le sole mie amare parole

Non lasciarmi ti prego
Sai quanto ami il tuo canto

Canto dell'amato

*CATVLLIANO CARMINE LI
ET SAPPHICO FRAGMENTO XXXI AFFLATVM*

He is sitting by you
Watching
Listening to your sweetest laughter

As if he were god
Even more than god in my eyes

It takes from me every sense of life

When I watch you
Saffic lover
Outside your womb
Nothing remains to me

Not even the words

Faint tongues of fire pervade me
Inside

My ears resonate with darkest sounds
My eyes are covered by night

Twofold shade

A frigid shiver of sweat
Takes control of my body
Now pallid

And death
Does not appear far

Inspired by Poem 51 by Gaivs Valerivs Catullus
and by Fragment 31 by Sappho

APVD LATVS TVVM CONSIDIT
TE SPECTAT
AVDIT RISVM TVVM DVLCISSIMVM

PAR DEO
SVPERIOR IPSO DEO

OMNES VITAE SENSVS MIHI ERIPIT

SIMVL TE ASPICIO
SAPPHICA AMANS
FORIS GREMIVM TVVM
NIHIL EST MI

NE VOX QVIDEM

TENVIS FLAMMA DEMANAT
SVB ARTVS

SONITV GRAVISSIMO TINTINANT AVRES
TEGVNTVR LVMINA NOCTE

GEMINA VMBRA

TREMOR SVDORE GELIDVS
CORPVS MEVM OCCVPAT
IAM LIVIDVM

ET MORS
NON LONGINQVA VIDETVR MI

*CATVLLIANO CARMINE LI
ET SAPPHICO FRAGMENTO XXXI AFFLATVM*

Si siede al tuo fianco
Ti guarda
Ascolta il tuo ridere dolcissimo

Come se fosse dio
Superiore a dio stesso ai miei occhi

Mi deruba di ogni senso di vita

Quando io ti guardo
Saffica amante
Fuori dal tuo grembo
Nulla più mi rimane

Neppure le parole

Lingue di fuoco tenui mi pervadono
Dentro

Le orecchie eccheggiano di suoni cupissimi
Gli occhi sono coperti da notte

Ombra duplice

Un tremore gelido di sudore
Si impadronisce del mio corpo
Ormai terreo

E la morte
Non sembra a me lontana

*Ispirato al Carme LI di Gaivs Valerivs Catvllvs
Ed al Frammento XXXI di Saffo*

CATVLLIANO CARMINE CI AFFLATVM

Through many countries
Through lands
And seas
I finally come to you
My brother

To give you the last tribute
And seated near your stone
Speak to your silent ashes

The olive trees of your garden
Recite your verses
In the calm of noon

Only with you
I would have wished to speak
And with you
Share everything
If only fortune would have allowed it

Accept my offering of sorrow
And these tears of fraternal crying

Farewell
My brother
Rest forever

I will jealously protect your words

Inspired by Poem 101 by Gaivs Valerivs Catullus

MVLTAS PER GENTES
PER TERRAS
ET AEQVORA
TANDEM AD TE ADVENIO
FRATER MI

VT TE POSTREMO DONAREM MVNERE
ET LAPIDI TVO ASSIDENS
MVTAM ALLOQVERER CINEREM

HORTI TVI OLEAE
VERSVS TVOS RECITANT
IN TRANQVILLITATE MERIDIEI

CVM TE SOLVM
VOLVISSEM LOQVI
ET TECVM
OMNIA COMMVNICARE
SI MODO FORTVNA ID CONCESSĪSSET

ACCIPE MVNVS MEVM MAERORIS
ET HAS LACRIMAS FRATERNO EX FLETV

ATQVE IN PERPETVVM
FRATER MI
AVE ATQVE VALE

DILIGENTISSIMA CVRA PROTEGAM VERBA TVA

CATVLLIANO CARMINE CI AFFLATVM

Attraverso molti popoli
Attraverso terre
E mari
Finalmente vengo a te
Fratello mio

Per donarti l'ultimo tributo
E seduto accanto alla tua pietra
Parlare con le tue ceneri silenziose

Gli ulivi del tuo giardino
Recitano i tuoi versi
Nella quiete del meriggio

Solo con te
Avrei voluto parlare
E con te
Condividere tutto
Se la fortuna lo avesse solo concesso

Accetta la mia offerta di dolore
E queste lacrime di pianto fraterno

Ti saluto
Fratello mio
Riposa per sempre

Proteggero' gelosamente le tue parole

Ispirato al Carme CI di Gaivs Valerivs Catvllvs

SPORAE

Thin grass
Adorns
With pearls of dew
Your foot pale of moon

My beloved

You come close

With ashen fingers
You offer the stem of a chalice

I touch it

Anthers loaded with pollen
Pour their sweetest nectar

Spores
Delicate and pure

Instinctive

The spores of a god

Spores

HERBA SVBTILIS
RORE RECENTI
GEMMAT
PALLIDVM PEDEM TVVM LVNAE

AMATA MEA

ADPROPINQVAS

CEREIS DIGITIS
MI CAVLEM CALICIS PRAEBES

ID TANGO

ANTHERAE POLMINE GRAVES
DOLCISSIMVM NECTAR EFFVNDVNT

SPORAS
LEVES ET PVRAS

NATVRALES

SPORAS DEI

SPORAE

Erba sottile
Di acerba rugiada
Imperla
Il tuo piede pallido di luna

Mia amata

Ti avvicini

Con dita ceree
Mi porgi lo stelo di un calice

Lo tocco

Antere cariche di polline
Riversano il loro nettare dolcissimo

Spore
Lievi e pure

Istintive

Le spore di un dio

Spore

REPERCVSSVS

Elea
Ecstatic calm of motionless late noons

An immense solitude
Describes the sacerdotal chastity

Aureate of declining sun
Grazing light opens the immensity of obscurity among the interstices of
the sacred colonnade

Not to them hostile

For an instant
Unveils bitter words in opaque gold
Weaves the weft of their physicality

Refracts through the reclined visage
Of the hieratic intensity
In androgynous masculinity

Unspeakable new power

Revolutionary staticity
In ambiguous transparence

Of verdigris

Refractions

ELEA
TARDI MERIDIEI IMMOTI ELATA TRANQVILLITAS

INGENS SOLITVDO
SACERDOTALEM CASTITATEM DESCRIBIT

OCCIDENTE SOLE INAVRATA
RADENS LVX IN SACRI COLVMNARVM ORDINIS
INTERVALLIS IMMENSITATEM TENEBRARVM APERIT

NON EIS ADVERSA

PER MOMENTVM TEMPORIS
AMARA VERBA NON PERLVCIDO AVRO MANIFESTA FACIT
TEXIT EORVM MATERIEI TRAMAM

PER VVLTVM RECLINATVM
SACERDOTALI VI
IN ANDROGYNA VIRILITATE REFRINGIT

NOVA INENARRABILIS POTENTIA

SEDITIOSA IMMOBILITAS
AMBIGVA PERLVCIDITATE

VIRIDIS

REPERCVSSVS

Elea
Calma estatica di tardi meriggi immoti

Una solitudine immensa
Descrive la castita' sacerdotale

Indorata di sole declinante
Luce radente tra gli interstizii del colonnato sacro apre l'immensita'
delle tenebre

Non a loro avversa

Per un istante
Rivela parole amare in oro opaco
Tesse la trama della loro matericita'

Rifrange attraverso il viso reclinato
Dall'intensita' ieratica
In androgina mascolinita'

Indicibile nuova potenza

Staticita' rivoluzionaria
In trasparenza ambigua

Di viride

Rifrazioni

DE SOLITVDINE

Night of anxiety

Beyond the obscurity of senses
I feel the urban pulse of distant sounds

Coordinated in orgiastic dissonance

Reverberating on the damp cobblestone
Of a devastated Berlin
Now bloodless

Mute of wind

Light reflected by unquiet clouds of violet
Reveals
Cold tears of unrestrained sweat

My lost limbs
Hardened by acre spasms

Most bitter

I perceive the beating of the wrist
Always felt as intimate violence

As unique extreme act which can still reconnect me with the matter

The tenuous coldness of existence

Solitude

NOX ANXIETATIS

SENSVVM VLTRA TENEBRAS
PVLSVM VRBANVM LONGINQVORVM SONORVM SENTIO

IN EFFRENATA VOCE DISSONA COMPOSITORVM

REPERCVTERE IN VDIIS VIIS SILICIS
DEVASTATI BEROLINI
IAM EXANGVIS

VENTO MVTI

REMISSA LVX INQVIETARVM NVBIVM VIOLACEARVM
PATEFACIT
FRIGIDAS LACRIMAS CONCITATO SVDORE

MEMBRA MEA DEERRATA
RIGIDA ASPERIS SPASMIS

AMARISSIMIS

ANIMADVERTO VENARVM PVLSVM
AB AETERNO QVASI INTIMAM VIM PERCEPTVM

VT SOLVM FACINVS EXTREMVM QVOD ME MATERIEI
COLLIGET

TENVI FRIGORI VITAE

DE SOLITVDINE

Notte di ansieta'

Oltre l'oscurita' dei sensi
Sento il pulsare urbano di suoni lontani

Coordinati in dissonanza orgiastica

Riverberare sul selciato umido
Di una Berlino devastata
Ormai esangue

Muta di vento

Luce riflessa di irrequiete nubi di viola
Rivela
Fredde lacrime di convulso sudore

Le mie membra smarrite
Irrigidite di crampi aspri

Amarissimi

Avverto il battito del polso
Da sempre percepito come intima violenza

Come unico estremo atto che ancora mi ricolleghi alla matericita'

Al tenue gelo dell'esistenza

Solitudine

VMOR

I roam

Streets worn out by obscene drugs
Consumed by betrayed childhoods

By corrupted generations

Still silver dampness
Under my bare feet

Stripped of original purity
The violence in my eyes

As silent dancer

Spreads an irrepressible hate
Within gazes of shadow

Until devoid of senses
The day is reborn

In radical sloth

Dampness

ERRO

PER VIAS OBSCENIS AROMATIS EXESAS
PVERITIIS PRODITIS CONSVMPTAS

CORRVPTIS GENERIBVS

ADHVC ARGENTEVS VMOR
SVB MEIS NVDIS PEDIBVS

INNATA CASTITATE PRIVATA
VIS IN OCVLIS MEIS

VT SILENS SALTATRIX

IMPLACABILE ODIVM DISSEMINAT
IN EX VMBRA ASPECTIBVS

DVM SINE SENSIBVS
IN IMMODICA IGNAVIA

DIES RENASCITVR

VMOR

Mi aggiro

Su strade logorate da droghe oscene
Consumate da infanzie tradite

Da generi imbastarditi

Ancora umidore argenteo
Sotto i miei piedi nudi

Privata della purezza originale
La violenza nei miei occhi

Quale danzatrice silenziosa

Dissemina un odio inestinguibile
Entro sguardi di ombra

Finche' senza sensi
Il giorno rinasce

In radicale accidia

Umidore

POETA

You call me poet

My word faces the silence in precarious balance
Quivers
Reflects its own vacuity

Poet you say

I have no name

I look for my word
Consumed

Behind tearful windows of glass
Among infirm solitudes

I read her reflected in the melancholic mirror
Of Corazzini

Poet

ME DICIS POETAM

VERBVM MEVM PARI MOMENTO LIBRATVM IN SILENTIO
APPARET
TREPIDAT
REPERCVTIT SVAM INANITATEM

POETAM DICIS

NVLLVM NOMEN EST MIHI

QVAERO VERBVM MEVM
CONSVMPTVM

POST VITRA LACRIMANTIA
IN AEGRIS SOLITVDINIBVS

ID LEGO REPERCVSSVM IN MAESTO SPECVLO
CORATINII

POETA

Mi dici poeta

La mia parola si affaccia in bilico sul silenzio
Freme
Riverbera della propria vacuita'

Poeta dici

Io non ho nome

Cerco la mia parola
Consumata

Dietro vetri lacrimosi
Fra solitudini malate

La leggo riflessa nello specchio melanconico
Di Corazzini

Poeta

CORRVPTVS EPHEBVS

Thin fingers
Of long gaunt hands
Beat the timpani of Dindymon

Celebrate a darkest sensuality

Fibers of impure linen
Coarse
Tear

In threads undo the long hair

The skin pale of almonds exposes on the slim chest
The abdomen slender
The thin hips

Immense nudity

An unrestrained violent dance
Ecstatic
Orgiastic
Overcomes me

Corruption of moments
Paroxysmal instant
Excruciating lucidity of acute senses

P a u s e

The ritual of masculine blood

Through pain
I assume every state of existence

I at one time child

I ephebos

I then youth

Gathered the flowers of adolescence
I now finally another time

Woman

Fallen ephebos

SVBTILES DIGITI
LONGARVM GRACILIVMQVE MANVVM
PERCVTIVNT TYMPANA DINDYMI

OBSCVRISSIMAM LIBIDINEM CELEBRANT

FIBRAE LINI CORRVPTI
IMPOLITI
SE LACERANT

CAPILLVM PROMISSVM IN PRAETENVIBVS FILIS
EFFVNDVNT

CVTIS VT AMYGDALA CANDIDA SE EXPONIT IN EXILI
PECTORE
MACRO IN VENTRE
SVBTILIBVS IN ILIBVS

NVDVM CORPVS IMMENSVM

VEHEMENS SALTATIO VIOLENTA
DIVINO SPIRITV INFLATA
EFFRENATA
ME POSSIDET

TEMPORIS PVNCTORVM CORRVPTIO
MOMENTVM EXTREMVM
ATROX EXACVTORVM SENSVVM MENTIS ACIES

I N T E R V A L L V M

CRVORIS VIRILIS RITVS

DOLORE
OMNEM STATVM VITAE ADSVMO

EGO OLIM PVER

EGO EPHEBVS

EGO POSTEA IVVENIS

FLORIBVS IVVENTVTI COLLIGATIS
EGO NVNC RVRSVM AD VLTIMVM

MVLIER

CORRVPTVS EPHEBVS

Dita sottili
Di mani lunghe e scarne
Percuotono i timpani di Dindimo

Celebrano una sensualita' cupissima

Le fibre del lino impuro
Grezzo
Si lacerano

In filamenti disciolgono i lunghi capelli

La pelle candida di mandorle si espone sul petto esile
Il ventre asciutto
Le ilia sottili

Immensa nudita'

Una convulsa danza violenta
Estatica
Orgiastica
Mi possiede

Corruzione di attimi
Parossistico istante
Atroce lucidita' di acuiti sensi

P a u s a

Il rito del sangue virile

Attraverso il dolore
Assumo ogni stato dell'esistenza

Io un tempo bambino

Io efebo

Io poi giovane

Raccolti i fiori della giovinezza
Io ora finalmente di nuovo

Donna

Efebo decaduto

IRIDES

Approach
Your face of white lilium
In the tenuous air of vesper

By effused light illuminated

Observe
My viridescent iris
With yours trembling of indigo

Soaked of candid travertine
Of Roman baroque

Penetrate
My pupils
By unquietness dilated

Permeated of uncertain reflections of noble crimson liquor

Beyond the transparencies of suspended tears

Finally
Perceive

Me

Irides

ADMOVE
VVLTVM TVVM ALBIS LILIIS
IN TENVI AVRA VESPERI

LVCE EFFVSA INLVMINATA

INTVERE
IRIDEM MEAM VIRIDEM
TVA TREPIDA INDICO

MADIDA CANDIDO LAPIDE TIBVRTINO
BAROCI ROMANI

PENETRA
IN PVPILLAS MEAS
TREPIDATIONE DILATATAS

REPERCVSSIBVS INCERTIS
NOBILIS LIQVORIS COCCINEI IMBVTAS

PRAETER PENDENTIVM LACRIMARVM
PERLVCIDITATES

AD VLTIMVM
PERCIPE

ME

IRIDES

Avvicina
Il tuo volto di gigli bianchi
Nella tenue aura del vespero

Da effusa luce rischiarata

Osserva
La mia iride viridea
Con la tua trepida di indaco

Madida di candido travertino
Di barocco romano

Penetra
Le mie pupille
Di inquietudine dilatate

Intrise di incerti riverberi di nobile liquore cremisi

Oltre le trasparenze di lacrime sospese

Finalmente
Percepisci

Me

Iridi

ΚΟΥΡΟΣ

I come to you as nude pagan kouros
Purify me I implore you

Nourish me with amber falerno from your fragile lips

Kouros

VT NVDVS ΚΟΥΡΟΣ PAGANVS AD TE VENIO
PVRIFICA ME TE ORO

ALE ME SVCINO FALERNO SVBTILIBVS LABRIS TVIS

ΚΟΥΡΟΣ

Vengo a te quale nudo κοῦϱος pagano
Purificami ti prego

Nutrimi di ambrato falerno dalle tue labbra sottili

ΚΟΥΡΟΣ (Kouros)

PERSONA

A gentle wind
Flutters on the sweetest slope

A fine rain
Weaves
A fragile veil of pearls

On your face

Permeated

Of melancholy

Persona

MITIS AVRA
DOLCISSIMVM SVPER DECLIVE VOLITAT

PLVVIA SVBTILIS
TEXIT
VELVM MARGARITIS LEVE

IN TVO VVLTV

AD MEASTITIAM

COMPOSITO

PERSONA

Vento mite
Aleggia sul declivio dolcissimo

Una pioggia fine
Tesse
Un velo lieve di perle

Sul tuo volto

Atteggiato

Di tristezza

Persona

DÆMON

Original disorder
Pure excess
Interminable primordial violence

Completed the metamorphosis
I emerge from the immensity of darkness
Still imbued with obscure light

Of a primitive sensuality
I writhe
Obscene extreme pulse

My demonic plumes
Stretch out

Tremble

My electric eyes
Of perylene and cobalt

Illuminate

Palpitate

Radiate
An archaic vehemence
Vertiginous ecstatic rage

I am
The eternal splendour

The magnificent

The absolute

Demon

INNATVS TVMVLTVS
INTEMPERANTIA PVRA
INTERMINATA PRISTINA VIS

METAMORPHOSI PERFECTA
EX TENEBRARVM IMMENSITATE EMERGO
ADHVC OBSCVRA LVCE IMBVTVS

IN LIBIDINE PRIMA
OBSCENA IMPVLSIONE IMMODICA
ME DISTORQVEO

MEAE PLVMAE LVCIFERAE
SE EXTENDVNT

TREPIDANT

OCVLI MEI ELECTRICI
CAERVLEI ATQVE PERYLENEI

SE ILLVMINANT

PALPITANT

DIFFVNDVNT
VEHEMENTIAM VETEREM
FVROREM DIVINO SPIRITV INFLATVM

EGO SVM
PERPETVVS FVLGOR

MAGNIFICVS IPSE

ABSOLVTVS

DAEMON

Disordine originale
Puro eccesso
Interminabile primigenia violenza

Completata la metamorfosi
Emergo dall'immensita' di tenebre
Ancora imbevuto di luce oscura

Mi contorco
Di un sensualismo primitivo
Oscena pulsione estrema

Le mie lucifere piume
Si distendono

Fremono

I miei occhi elettrici
Di perilene e cobalto

Si illuminano

Palpitano

Irradiano
Una veemenza arcaica
Vertiginoso furore estatico

Io sono
L'eterno splendore

Il magnificente

L'assoluto

Demone

M M XVIII

The city impure covers with shadow

Willows in the twilight
The mute soil

Beyond the shroud
You
My brother

Your face reclined
The eyes unquiet

With faint voice
I tell you of us

Veiled an unspeakable anxiety

With a bitter smile
I tremble with poetry

In me
With me you breathe

Forever

My brother
Farewell

M M XVIII

IMPVRA VRBS VMBRA SE TEGIT

SALICES PRIMO VESPERE
MVTVM SOLVM

PRAETER VELVM
TV
FRATER MI

VVLTVS TVVS RECLINATVS
INQVIETI OCVLI

VOCE SVBMISSA
TIBI DE NOBIS NARRO

VELATA ANXIETATE INENARRABILI

AMARO CVM RISV
POESE TREMO

IN ME
CVM ME RESPIRAS

IN PERPETVVM

FRATER MI
VALE

M M XVIII

La citta' impura si copre d'ombra

Salici nel crepuscolo
Il suolo muto

Oltre il velario
Tu
Fratello mio

Il tuo volto reclinato
Gli occhi irrequieti

Con voce sommessa
Ti racconto di noi

Velata un' ansieta' inesprimibile

Con amaro sorriso
Tremo di poesia

In me
Con me respiri

Per sempre

Fratello mio
Addio

M M XVIII

CAERVLEA TREPIDATIO

Among the archaic walls
Water penetrates the soil
Copious

In the room fragrant of wreaths
A faint flame of Syrian oil
Trembles

Tenuous light
Caresses your skin

The dress of Ionian silk flows from your shoulders
To expose your polished sides
Of bronze

Falls at your feet

Fragile

Uncovers their delicate veins
Of the cobalt reflections

I kiss them gently

My lips resolve in light

Most pure

Blue tremble

VETERIBVS IN MVRIS
AQVA IN TERRAM PENETRAT
COPIOSA

IN CVBICVLO FRAGRANTI SERTIS
FLEBILIS FLAMMA SYRIACI OLEI
TREPIDAT

TENVE LVMEN
PERMVLCET TVAM CVTIM

IONICA VESTIS SERICA AB VMERIS FLVIT
NVDAT EXPOLITA LATERA
AENEA

DECIDIT PEDIBVS TVIS

EXILIBVS

DETEGIT EORVM TENVES VENAS
CAERVELIS REPERCVSSIBVS

EOS LEVITER BASIO

MEA LABRA IN LVCEM EVANESCVNT

PVRISSIMAM

CAERVLEA TREPIDATIO

Tra le arcaiche mura
L'acqua penetra la terra
Copiosa

Nella camera fragrante di ghirlande
Una flebile fiamma di olio di Siria
Freme

Tenue chiarore
Accarezza la tua pelle

La veste di seta ionia scorre dalle spalle
Scopre i fianchi levigati
Di bronzo

Cade ai tuoi piedi

Esili

Ne scopre le vene delicate
Dai riflessi di cobalto

Li bacio lievemente

Le mie labbra si risolvono in luce

Purissima

Fremito blu

PERLVCIDITATES

It rains on your aureate hair
Of the elegiac accents

Drawing ionic filigrees on your soft temples

I observe
The grace of their correspondences
Through the delicate veil spun by the winds

Woven of most fine light

Tears flow along your pure eyelashes
Adorned with poetry

They chase each other on your thin mouth

Then penetrate your trembling lips
Barely open

In them of inebriation I palpitate

Filigrees

PLVIT IN TVVM AVRATVM CAPILLVM
ACCENTIBVS ELEGIACIS

IONICIS PERLVCIDITATIBVS DELINEANDIS
IN TVIS TEMPORIBVS LEVIBVS

EARVM DVLCEDINEM CONGRVENTIVM
PER TENVE VELVM AVRIS INTEXTVM
INTVEOR

EX LVCE SVBTILISSIMA NEXVM

LACRIMAE FLVVNT PER TVA CILIA PVRISSIMA
POESE ORNATA

TVVM IN OS EXILE INSEQVVNTVR

POSTEA TVA LABRA TREPIDA PENETRANT
MODICE RECLVSA

IN IIS PER EBRIETATEM PALPITO

PERLVCIDITATES

Piove sui tuoi capelli aurati
Dagli accenti elegiaci

A disegnare ioniche filigrane sulle tempie lievi

Ne osservo
La grazia delle corrispondenze
Attraverso il velo leggiero intessuto dai venti

Tramato di luce finissima

Lacrime scorrono sulle tue ciglia intemerate
Orne di poesia

Si inseguono sulla tua bocca esile

Poi penetrano le tue trepide labbra
Appena dischiuse

Ne palpito di ebbrezza

Filigrane

NOX LETHAEA (detail)
Brushed Steel and LED Lights (23"x14"x2" · 58x36x5cm)

NOX LETHAEA (detail)
Brushed Steel and LED Lights (23"x14"x2" · 58x36x5cm)

FLVMEN

The poet observes

Listens

With feminine sensitivity assumes the impressions

And the fragile sense reemerges

Long letter
Solar restraint

And docile exchange

RIVER

By Marco Mathieu

POETA INTVETVR

AVSCVLTAT

FEMINEO SENSV MOTVS ADSVMIT

ET FRAGILIS SIGNIFICATIO ITERVM EMERGIT

LONGA EPISTVLA
SOLARE FRENVM

ATQVE DOCILIS PERMVTATIO

FLVMEN

Il poeta osserva

Ascolta

Con femminile sensibilita' assume le impressioni

Ed il fragile senso riemerge

Lettera lunga
Solare freno

E docile scambio

FIUME

Di Marco Mathieu

ANIMARVM MERGENTES

For us who are sitting here

Today

Whilst the time increases
The stories however do not

We thought certainties
We lived on contemporaneity

"We will always remember everything"
Then instead
Until the mirror closes its circle

The beats inside
The adrenalin rising

We remain what we are

Divers of souls

By Marco Mathieu

NOBIS HIC SEDENTIBVS

HODIE

DVM TEMPVS AVGETVR
NARRATIONES CONTRA MINIME

COGITABAMVS RES CERTAS
HOC DIE VIVEBAMVS

"OMNIA RECORDABIMVR"
POSTEA CONTRA
VSQVE TEMPVS IN QVO SPECVLVM CIRCVLVM SVVM
PERFICIT

PALPITATIONES INTVS
ADRENALINA CRESCIT

MANEMVS QVOD SVMVS

ANIMARVM MERGENTES

Per noi che stiamo qui seduti

Oggi

Mentre il tempo aumenta
I racconti invece no

Pensavamo certezze
Vivevamo di oggi

"Ricorderemo sempre tutto"
Poi invece
Fin quando lo specchio finisce il suo giro

I battiti dentro
L'adrenalina che sale

Rimaniamo quello che siamo

Tuffatori di anime

Di Marco Mathieu

EGO

No one is worse than me
I know the world

I desire and devour it
Observe
Endure

Love
Hate
Live and feel

Suffer

Demand and destroy

I

By Marco Mathieu

QVAM ME PEIOR NEMO EST
NOSCO MVNDVM

EVM CVPIO ET DEVORO
INTVEOR
PATIOR

AMO
ODI
VIVO ATQVE SENTIO

EXCRVCIOR

POSTVLO ET DELEO

EGO

Peggio di me non c'è nessuno
Conosco il mondo

Lo desidero e divoro
Osservo
Subisco

Amo
Odio
Vivo e sento

Soffro

Pretendo e distruggo

IO

Di Marco Mathieu

POESIS

ΠΟΙΗΣΙΣ

Apollonian fixedness
Of aestheticizing inclinations

Your words
Radiated by nocturnal tremors

Sprinkle

My pale body
Frail

Entirely naked

Laying on arid soil

I feel their cold dampness
On my ashen skin

In noble solitude
I crystallize them
In verses of the hieratic intensity

In subtle analogies
I illuminate

Poetry

ΠΟΙΗΣΙΣ

IMMOTAE APOLLINEAE INCLINATIONES
ARTIS

TVA VERBA
CIRCVMFVSA NOCTVRNIS TREPIDATIONIBVS

IRRORANT

MEVM CORPVS PALLIDVM
EXILE

PRORSVS NVDVM

IN ARIDA TERRA SVPINVM

SENTIO EORVM FRIGIDVM VMOREM
IN MEA CVTE CEREA

IN NOBILI SOLITVDINE
EA IN CRYSTALLVM DENSO
IN VERSIBVS VI SACERDOTALI

ME ILLVMINO
IN SVBTILIBVS ANALOGIIS

POESIS

ΠΟΙΗΣΙΣ

Fissita' apollinea
Di inclinazioni estetizzanti

Le tue parole
Irradiate da notturni fremiti

Irrorano

Il mio pallido corpo
Esile

Interamente ignudo

Su arida terra riverso

Ne avverto il freddo umidore
Sulla mia pelle cerea

In nobile solitudine
Le cristallizzo
In versi dall' intensita' ieratica

Di sottili analogie
M'illumino

Poesia

PATER

ΠΑΤΗΡ

From the reputation and memory of my father
Acrid pride and gentle blood

Unquietness of spirit and virile melancholy

Father

ΠΑΤΗΡ

EXISTIMATIONE ET RECORDATIONE PATRIS MEI
SVPERBIAM ACREM ET NOBILEM SANGVINEM

INQVIETVDINEM ANIMI
ATQVE VIRILEM AEGRITVDINEM

PATER

ΠΛΤΗΡ

Dalla reputazione e dalla memoria di mio padre
Acre orgoglio e sangue gentile

Inquietudine d'animo e virile malinconia

Padre

KORE

Gelid Kore
Of the shadow of snow

You surface from the haze of pearl
Which envelops
The necropolis of lovers

Dressed of silver
With the peplos untied

A wreath of barley
Wrapping your head

The wind smells of hyacinths
On the silent soil
Of decomposing leaves

With waxen fingers
Of your tapering hand
You penetrate my chest

You gather
The breath of the soul

I pray you

Bring to you my semi alive body
On the meadows of asphodel

Kore

FRIGIDA KORE
NIVEA VMBRA

EMERGIS EX ONYCHE CALIGINE
QVAE COMPLECTITVR
SEPVLCRETVM AMANTIVM

ARGENTO INDVTA
PEPLO SOLVTO

SERTO EX HORDEO
CAPITE CINGENTI

AVRA HYACINTHIS OLET
SVPRA TACITVRNVM SOLVM
EX MARCENTIBVS FOLIIS

CEREIS DIGITIS
TVAE TERETIS MANVS
IN MEVM PECTVS PENETRAS

SPIRITVM ANIMI
COGIS

TE ORO

DVCE TIBI MEVM CORPVS SEMIVIVVM
IN PRATIS ASPHODELI

KORE

Gelida Kore
Dalla nivea ombra

Emergi dalla bruma perlacea
Che avvolge
La necropoli degli amanti

Vestita d'argento
Con il peplo sciolto

Un serto di orzo
A cingerti il capo

Il vento aulisce di giacinti
Sul suolo taciturno
Di foglie marcescenti

Con ceree dita
Della tua mano affusolata
Mi penetri il petto

Raccogli
Il respiro dell'anima

Ti prego

Conduci con te il mio corpo semivivo
Sui prati d'asfodelo

Kore

FEBRIS VESPERTINA

Only with you
On desert islands of Diomedes
Most translucent

Surrounded by docile waters
Of sombre emerald
Darkening

Promontories of sandstone
Motionless
Of the intense scent of basil
Describe
The line of the sea

Discoloured
Of humid salt

The wind touches
My consumed eyelids
In eternity violated

Drained and emaciated
I prostrate at your feet
Pellucid

Embrace
My decadence

Liberate
My tormented shadow

Exhale
My life

Watch me rise again

Whilst in the rage of vesper
Alone we remain amongst mortals

Crepuscular fever

SOLVS TECVM
DESERTIS IN DIOMEDEIS INSVLIS
NITIDISSIMIS

DOCILIBVS AQVIS CIRCVMDATIS
ATRO SMARAGDO
SE OBSCVRANTIBVS

PROMVNTVRIA ARENARIA
IMMOTA
OCIMI VEHEMENTI ODORE
LINEAM MARIS
DESCRIBVNT

VMIDA SALSEDINE
COLOREM MVTATAM

AVRA LEVITER ADTINGIT
MEAS PALPEBRAS CONSVMPTAS
IN PERPETVVM VIOLATAS

ADTRITVS ET MACIE CONFECTVS
ME AD PEDES TVOS PROSTERNO
PERLVCIDOS

AMPLECTERE
MEVM OCCASVM

LIBERA
MEAM EXCRVCIATAM VMBRAM

EXHALA
ANIMAM MEAM

INTVERE ME IN VITAM REDEVNTEM

DVM IN VI VESPERI
SOLI INTER MORTALES SVMVS

FEBRIS VESPERTINA

Solo con te
Su deserte isole Diomedee
Tersissime

Circondate da acque docili
Di atro smeraldo
Oscurantesi

Promontori arenarii
Immoti
Dall'intenso profumo di basilico
Descrivono
La linea del mare

Trascolorata
Di umida salsedine

Il vento tocca
Le mie palpebre consunte
In eterno violate

Logoro ed emaciato
Mi prostro ai tuoi piedi
Perlucidi

Abbraccia
La mia decadenza

Libera
La mia ombra tormentata

Esala
La mia vita

Guardami risorgere

Mentre nel furore del vespro
Soli restiamo fra i mortali

Febbre crepuscolare

AD VITAM REDITVS

The tenuous line of light of dawn
A diffused beauty

Absolute love · Her love

Rebirth

TENVIS LINEA LVCIS AVRORAE
PVCHRITVDO DIFFVSA

ABSOLVTVS AMOR · EIVS AMOR

AD VITAM REDITVS

La tenue linea di luce dell'aurora
Una bellezza diffusa

Amore assoluto · Il suo amore

Rinascita

FEMINEA AVRORA (detail)
Steel, Cast Crystal and LED Lights (18"x11"x11" · 45x28x28cm)

FEMINEA AVRORA (detail)
Steel, Cast Crystal and LED Lights (18"x11"x11" · 45x28x28cm)

HVMVS ET LVX

I am generated by humus
Soaked acrid soil
Ignoble

Slowly I stand

The feet sink in the tepid ground
Drenched with my dark blood

Coagulated
In putrefying obscure matter

My unquiet soul
Observes

The power of expression
Of the Lydian flautist

Is reborn in its slow iterative melody
Archaic
Original

In the supreme orgy
Of imperfect bodies

The Dionysian sense
Structures a protracted metamorphosis

Transmutes the lineaments

The forehead vast

The nose thin
The skin waxen

The appearance of a god
Pale of light

The sun eventually emerges
On the endless silent fields

Amongst the arid ears
Of aureate wheat

Splendid
Obscured gold

Humus and Light

HVMO GIGNOR
MADIDA TERRA ASPERA
IGNOBILI

LENTE SVRGO

PEDES IN TEPIDO SOLO SVBMERGVNT
OBSCVRO CRVORE MEO INBVTO

COAGVLATO
IN OBSCVRISSIMA PVTRETVDINE

MEA ANIMA INQVIETA
INTVETVR

POTENTIAM SIGNIFICATIONIS
AVLOEDI LYDII

RENASCITVR IN EIVS MELOPOEIA LENTA
VETERE
PRIMA

IN SVPREMIS ORGIIS
CORPORVM IMPERFECTORVM

SENSVS DIONYSIACVS
LONGINQVAM FORMAE MVTATIONEM EXPRIMIT

LINEAMENTA NOVAT

FRONTEM AMPLAM

SVBTILEM NASVM
CVTIM CEREAM

ASPECTVS DEI
LVCIS CANDIDI

SOL AD VLTIMVM EMERGIT
SVPER INTERMINATOS TACITOS AGROS

IN SPICAS ARIDAS
FRVMENTI AVREI

FVLGENS
INVMBRATVM AVRVM

HVMVS ET LVX

Sono generato dall'umo
Madida terra aspra
Ignobile

Lentamente mi ergo

I piedi affondano nel suolo tiepido
Intriso del mio sangue cupo

Coagulato
In putretudine scurissima

La mia anima inquieta
Osserva

La potenza d'espressione
Del flautista Lidio

Rinasce nella sua melopea lenta
Arcaica
Originaria

Nell'orgia suprema
Di corpi imperfetti

Il senso dionisiaco
Articola una protratta metamorfosi

Trasmuta i lineamenti

La fronte vasta

Il naso sottile
La pelle cerea

L'aspetto di un dio
Candido di luce

Il sole alfine affiora
Sugli interminati agri taciti

Fra spighe aride
Di grano dorato

Splendido
Adombrato oro

Umo e Luce

VESTIGIVM

Remissive sand

Transient impression
Of your light step

Impression

OBSEQVENS ARENA

VESTIGIVM FRAGILE
LEVIS GRADVS TVI

VESTIGIVM

Sabbia remissiva

Fugace impressione
Del tuo leggiero passo

Impressione

IMAGO

I observe the depth of sorrow

Protected by the illusion
Of my fragile skin

Illusion

SVMMVM DOLOREM INTVEOR

FRAGILIS CVTIS MEAE
FALSA IMAGINE PROTECTVS

IMAGO

Osservo la profondita' del dolore

Protetto dall'illusione
Della mia fragile pelle

Illusione

AVREORVM MALORVM SILVA

Born to one only life

I have been waiting for you since the beginning of time
Since the fragrant orange grove
Of primordial chaos

I have always known the lines of your soft hands

The texture of the reliefs of their frail veins

The reflection of the moon
On your pupils moist and chaste

The grace of your elegant gesture

Adored Erato

Cherished not as a lover his beloved
But as a father loves each one of his children

As offer I bring you my verses
Reflected by the gold of the mosaics of Byzantium

Vain presents
Of a pale poet

Imperfect signs
Of a non transmissible soul

Fragrant orange grove

AD VNAM VITAM NATVS

EX INITIO TEMPORIS TE EXPECTAVI
EX SILVA AVREORVM MALORVM FRAGRANTI
EX PRIMO CHAO

EX PERPETVO
MOLLIVM MANVVM TVARVM LINEAS ADGNOSCO
TRAMAM EMINENTIVM EARVM TENVIVM VENARVM

REPERCVSSVM LVNAE
IN VDIS ET CASTIS PVPILLIS TVIS

ELEGANTIS GESTVS TVI SVAVITATEM

CARISSIMA 'ΕΡΑΤΩ

DILECTA NON TANTVM VT VVLGVS AMICAM
SED PATER VT GNATOS DILIGIT ET GENEROS

DONVM TIBI VERSVS MEOS CONFERO
AVRO MVSIVORVM BYZANTII REPERCVSSOS

VANA MVNERA
PALLIDI POETAE

IMPERFECTA SIGNA
ANIMAE INCOMMVNICABILIS

AVREORVM MALORVM SILVA

Nato a una sola vita

Ti ho attesa dall'inizio del tempo
Dall' aranceto odoroso
Del caos primordiale

Da sempre conosco le linee delle tue morbide mani
La trama dei rilievi delle loro esili vene

Il riflesso della luna
Sulle tue pupille umide e caste

La grazia del tuo elegante gesto

Erato adorata

Diletta non come un amante l'amata
Ma come un padre ama ognuno dei suoi figli

Ti porto in offerta i miei versi
Riflessi dall'oro dei mosaici di Bisanzio

Vani doni
Di un pallido poeta

Segni imperfetti
Di un'anima intrasmissibile

Aranceto odoroso

CARTHAGO

In verses
I describe Carthago's final day

The crying of the beloved Elyssa
The sorrow
The anguish

The separation

The sight of the recomposed corpse
Dinstant
On the Lybian coast

Of the trembling aura
Turbid
Which encircles the funeral pyre

Curdles my blood

My dilated eyes
Conceal
The inner crying

Outside your womb
I don't feel belonging
My queen

Your words rain on me
In liturgical melody

As bitter ash

Carthago

IN VERSIBVS
DESCRIBO EXTREMVM DIEM CARTHAGINIS

DILECTAE ELISSAE FLETVM
DOLOREM
ANGOREM

LONGINQVITATEM

COMPOSITI CORPORIS SPECIES
AMOTI
LIBYCIS IN LITORIBVS

AVREAE VEHEMENTIS
TVRBIDAE
FVNEBREM PYRAM CIRCVMVOLVENTIS

SANGVINEM MEVM GELAT

OCVLI MEI DILATATI
CELANT
INTERIOREM FLETVM

EXTRA GREMBVM TVVM
CONIVNCTIONEM NON SENTIO
REGINA MEA

VERBA TVA IN ME PLVVNT
VT MELOPOEIA

QVASI AMARA CINIS

CARTHAGO

In versi
Descrivo il giorno finale di Cartagine

Il pianto dell'amata Elissa
La sofferenza
L'angoscia

La lontananza

La vista del cadavere ricomposto
Longinquo
Sulle coste libiche

Dell'aura vibrante
Torbida
Che avvolge la pira funeraria

Mi gela il sangue

I miei occhi dilatati
Celano
Il pianto interiore

Fuori dal tuo grembo
Non sento appartenenza
Mia regina

Le tue parole su me piovono
In melopea

Quale cenere amara

Cartagine

NOS

In lagoon of light
By glares of silver caressed

As veiled lovers

We

IN PALVDE EX LVCE
REPERCVSSIBVS ARGENTEIS BLANDITA

TAMQVAM VELATI AMANTES

NOS

In laguna di luce
Da riflessi di argento blandita

Quali velati amanti

NΩ (Noi)

OCEANVS

At the ends of the earth
Ocean talks to me

A vehemence of wave deafens the air

I savour
Your mouth of lilium

Soaked
Of sweetest fragrance

I search its evanescent traces
On my pale fingers

In pure sensuality
I palpitate

In you
Glaucous light of a moon of brume

I breathe

Ocean

IN FINIBVS TERRAE
OCEANVS MI LOQVITVR

VEHEMENTIA VNDAE AEREM OBTVNDIT

GVSTO
LILIACEVM OS TVVM

DVLCI EFFVSO ODORE
IMBVTVM

EVANESCENTIA EIVS VESTIGIA QVAERO
IN MEIS PALLIDIS DIGITIS

PVRA LIBIDINE
FLAGRO

IN TE
GLAVCO LVMINE CALIGINOSAE LVNAE

RESPIRO

OCEANVS

Ai confini della terra
Oceano mi parla

Una veemenza d'onda assorda l'aria

Assaporo
La tua bocca liliacea

Di dolcissimo effluvio
Imbevuta

Ne cerco le evanescenti tracce
Sulle mie pallide dita

Di pura sensualita'
Palpito

In te
Glauca luce di luna brumosa

Respiro

Oceano

SAPPHICVM FRAGMENTVM CLXVIII

The moon has set, as have the Pleiades
In the middle of the night I the feel time passing slowly

And I sleep still alone

Poetic translation of Fragment CLXVIII by Sappho

Δέδυκε μὲν ἀ σελάννα
καὶ Πληίαδες· μέσαι δὲ
νύκτες, παρὰ δ' ἔρχετ' ὤρα,
ἔγω δὲ μόνα κατεύδω

SAPPHICVM FRAGMENTVM CLXVIII

La luna e' tramontata, come le Pleiadi
Nel mezzo della notte sento il tempo trascorrere lentamente

Ed io dormo ancora sola

Traduzione poetica del Frammento CLXVIII di Saffo

AMYGDALA

You approach me
Orned with garlands of white apple flowers

Immodest

You tear the peplos of ashen linen
Fragrant of Assyrian myrrh

Exposing the virginal breast
Florid

The minuteness of the waxen hip

The silken groin of the tenuous almond fuzz

You pretend to be submissive

Consumed by the fire of lust
Corrupt uncontrollable turgidness

Purple under your skin

Almond

ADPROPINQVAS
SERTIS CANDIDIS FLORIBVS MALI CINCTA

IMPVDICA

PEPLVM ALBO LINO DISCINDIS
MYRRHIS ASSYRIIS FRAGRANS

AD VIRGINALEM SINVM REVELANDVM
TVRGIDVM

CEREI LATERIS EXIGVITATEM

MOLLE INGVEN TENVI AMYGDALAE LANVGINE

MODESTA SIMVLAS

CONSVMPTA IGNE LIBIDINIS
IMMVNDO EFFRENATO TVMORE

SVB CVTE VIOLACEO

AMYGDALA

Ti avvicini
Cinta di ghirlande di candidi fiori di melo

Impudica

Discindi il peplo di albo lino
Fragrante di mirre assire

A scoprire il seno verginale
Rigonfio

L'esiguita' dell'anca cerea

L'inguine morbido dalla tenue peluria di mandorla

Ti fingi remissiva

Consumata dal fuoco della lussuria
Immondo infrenabile turgore

Viola sotto la pelle

Mandorla

INQVIETVM OTIVM

Poetry
Nocturnal art

Unquiet idleness

In light fever dresses me with paleness

Verses of ancient writers
Accompany me to unusual regions

As palpitating shadows

Whilst steam dissolves
Around the nude shoulders
In abandoned slowness

As pale poet
In tremor of word
I assume the modulations of the hour

I transfigure the silence of things
In hieratic intensity

Obscure senses of unheard opulence

Until in lyrical moment

The lips parts the breath

Unquiet idleness

POESIS
ARS NOCTVRNA

INQVIETVM OTIVM

LEVI IN FEBRI ME PALLORE VESTIT

ANTIQVORVM VERSVS SCRIPTORVM
AD INSVETAS REGIONES ME DVCVNT

VT VMBRAE PALPITANTES

DVM VAPOR EVANESCIT
IN PROIECTA LENITATE
CIRCA VMEROS NVDOS

SICVT EXANGVIS POETA
IN TREPIDATIONE VERBI
ADSVMO MODVLATIONES HORAE

MVTO TACITVRNITATEM RERVM
IN VIM SACERDOTALEM

SENSVS OBSCVRI OPVLENTIAE INAVDITAE

DVM IN LYRICVM TEMPORIS MOMENTVM

SPIRITVS LABRA RECLVDIT

INQVIETVM OTIVM

Poesia
Arte notturna

Inquieto ozio

In febbre leggiera mi veste di pallore

I versi di scrittori antichi
Mi accompagnano in insuete regioni

Quali ombre palpitanti

Mentre il vapore si dissolve
Attorno alle spalle nude
In abbandonata lentezza

Quale esangue poeta
In fremiti di parola
Assumo le modulazioni dell'ora

Trasfiguro la taciturnita' delle cose
In intensita' ieratica

Oscuri sensi di opulenza inaudita

Finche' in momento lirico

Le labbra schiude il respiro

Ozio inquieto

SINDON

At the limits of the desert
The phebean light of crepuscule
Oblique
Caresses
Bitter tamarices

Lightly touches
The inviolable circle
Of the sepulchres of the Atreides

Reveals their tenuous imperfections
The clayey impurities
The coarse surface

Under a veil of tears
My lips
Cracked
Consumed by the sun
Stroke
The raw linen of your shroud
Covered with ashes

The wind of Mycenae
Interrupts the sepulchral silence

Intermits to the ecstatic calm
The acrid tedium of distant lamentations
Obsessive choral implorations

Whilst in exile
Alone
In the tacit soil

Your adored mouth
Withers

Shroud

SOLITVDINVM IN FINIBVS
PHOEBEA LVX CREPVSCVLI
OBLIQVA
AMARAS MYRICAS
BLANDITVR

LEVITER
INVIOLABILEM CIRCVLVM ATRIDARVM
ATTINGIT

EIVS TENVIA VITIA PATEFACIT
IMPVRITATES ARGILLOSAS
SCABRAM SVPERFICIEM

SVB VELO FLETV
LABRA MEA
LACERATA
SOLE EXESA
PERMVLCENT
IMPOLITVM LINVM SINDONIS TVAE
CINERE SPARSAE

VENTVS MYCENARVM
SEPVLCHRALE SILENTIVM INTERRVMPIT

ACRE TAEDIVM LONGINQVARVM LAMENTATIONVM
ANXIARVM IMPLORATIONVM CHORI
ELATAE TRANQVILLITATI INTERMITTIT

DVM IN EXILIO
SOLVM
IN TACITA TERRA

TVVM OS DILECTVM
VIESCIT

SINDON

Ai confini del deserto
La luce febea del crepuscolo
Obliqua
Blandisce
Amare tamerici

Lievemente sfiora
Il cerchio inviolabile
Dei sepolcri degli Atridi

Ne rivela le tenui imperfezioni
Le impurita' argillose
La superficie scabra

Sotto un velo di pianto
Le mie labbra
Screpolate
Consumate dal sole
Carezzano
Il lino grezzo della tua sindone
Coperta di ceneri

Il vento di Micene
Interrompe il silenzio sepolcrale

Intermette alla calma estatica
Il tedio acre di lontane lamentazioni
Ossessive implorazioni corali

Mentre in esilio
Sola
Nella terra taciturna

La tua adorata bocca
Disfiora

Sindone

SVLAMITIS

I listen to the rain beating the white sand

Touching rhythmically
The silver plain
Of the sea of Tiberias

Fingers of ivory play the lyre
Diffuse melodies of oranges and amber
Moved by the gentle breath of the valley of Megiddo

Amongst pale silent sheets
An immeasurable solitude
Seduces me

I miss you
Most gentle Shulammite

Loved by your mother
As no one has ever been

I miss
Your lovable aspect
Wrapped by the golden filigrees of Bactria

The attraction of your refined word

The elegance of your noble gesture

Bring me
The frail veins of cobalt of your virgin eyelids

You see
They demand to be reflected
By the delicate moisture on my lips

Shulammite

ARENAM CANDIDAM PERCVTIENTEM IMBREM AVSCVLTO

MODVLATE TANGENTEM
AEQVOR ARGENTEVM
LACVS TIBERIADIS

EBVRNEI DIGITI LYRA CANVNT
DIFFVNDVNT AVREI MALI ELECTRIQVE CANTVS
LEVI AVRA VALLIS MAGEDDI MOTOS

CANDIDIS IN LINTEIS TACITIS
INGENS SOLITVDO
SEVOCAT ME

MIHI DEEST
DVLCISSIMA SVLAMITIS

A MATRE TVA AMATA
VT NVLLA VMQVAM FVERIT

MIHI DEEST
FORMA TVA AMABILIS
AVREORVM FILORVM GRANO BACTRIAE CINCTA

TVAE PERPOLITAE VOCIS SVAVITAS

ELEGANTIA TVI PRETIOSI GESTVS

ADFER MIHI
TVARVM PALPEBRARVM CERVLEAS EXILES VENAS

VIDES
MEORVM VMORE LABRORVM
REPERCVTIENDI INDIGENT

SVLAMITIS

Ascolto la pioggia battere la sabbia bianca

Toccare ritmicamente
La piana argentea
Del lago di Tiberiade

Dita d'avorio suonano la lira
Diffondono melodie d'arancia e d'ambra
Mosse dall'aura lieve della valle di Megiddo

Fra candide lenzuola silenziose
Un'immensurabile solitudine
Mi rapisce

Mi manchi
Dolcissima Shulammite

Amata da tua madre
Come nessuna lo sia mai stata

Mi manca
Il tuo amabile aspetto
Cinto dalle filigrane d'oro di Bactria

L'incanto della tua parola raffinata

L'eleganza del tuo nobile gesto

Portami
Le esili vene di cobalto delle tue palpebre vergini

Vedi
Hanno bisogno di essere riflesse
Dall'umidore dalle mie labbra

Shulammite

SACERDOS

Dunes of clay sand in the wind of Buran
Effuse
Vivid fragrances of Bactria

Most noble nomadic woman
Priestess of Ahura Mazda

As purple ribbon
Your lips
Ooze a virgin nectar

Of elegance suffused

Lavender oil
Pale of violet
Spreads its intense essence

Soothes the skin of your pure neck
Pellucid
Adorned with red sea pearls

Tears quiver on the fingers
At the pulsation of the nostrils

A pause

The juice of my pomegranate
Produces an aromatic Achaemenid wine

Drink it I beg you
Its purity caresses your gaze

Priestess

ARENAE EX ARGILLA IN SARMATICO VENTO
EFFVNDVNT
VIVIDOS ODORES BACTRIAE

NOBILIS ERRANS MVLIER
SACERDOS OROMAZIS

VT PVRPVREVS LEMNISCVS
TVA LABRA
VIRGINALE MEL STILLANT

ELEGANTIA SVFFVSVM

OLEVM LAVANDVLAE
VIOLA PALLIDVM
EIVS ACRES ODORES SPARGIT

PERMVLCET PELLEM TVI PVRI COLLI
PERLVCIDI
MARGARITIS MARIS RVBRI ADORNATI

PALPITANTIBVS NARIBVS
LACRIMAE IN DIGITIS TREPIDANT

MORA

SVCVS MALI PVNICAE MEAE
ACHAEMENIDARVM PROCREAT OLENS VINVM

BIBE TE ORO
EIVS SINCERITAS ASPECTVI TVO BLANDITVR

SACERDOS

Le dune di sabbia argilla nel vento di Buran
Effondono
Accesi profumi di Bactria

Nobile donna nomade
Sacerdotessa di Ahura Mazda

Quale nastro di porpora
Le tue labbra
Stillano miele vergine

Di eleganza soffuso

Olio di lavanda
Pallido di viola
Spande la sua essenza intensa

Addolcisce la pelle del tuo collo puro
Perlucido
Adornato di perle del mar rosso

Lacrime sulle dita fremono
Al palpitare delle narici

Una pausa

Il succo del mio melograno
Produce un aromatico vino achemenide

Bevi ti prego
La sua purezza blandisce il tuo sguardo

Sacerdotessa

PHOEBEVS FVROR

The incandescent sky
Illuminates
The slow marble of waters

The horses of the sun
Maned of impetuous violence
Bring the wrath of Apollo

Phebean light cuts through the darkness

The destroyer God
The Obscure
Generated by Leto of the beautiful hair

Irate in his heart
With the bow of silver
In vibration of arrows

Massacres

For nine days
On the field of crimson poppies

As a bed of Danaid blood
Under the feet the earth mourns sombre

Amongst obscene altars
The pyres burn
Dense

The Punisher
Drinks their flames

In eyes white of ire

Phebean wrath

CANDENS CAELVM
ILLVMINAT
LENE MARMOR AQVARVM

EQVI SOLIS
VEHEMENTIS VIOLENTIAE CRINITI
APOLLINEVM FVROREM FERVNT

PHOEBEA LVX VMBRAM PARTĪTVR

EVERSOR DEVS
ΛΟΞΙΑΣ OBSCVRVS
A LATONA PVLCHRA COMA PARTVS

ANIMO IRATVS
ARCV ARGENTEO
TELORVM FREMITV

CAEDEM FACIT

NOVEM PER DIES
IN COCCINEORVM PAPAVERVM AGRO

VT CRVORIS DANAORVM LECTVS
SVB PEDIBVS TERRA TRISTIS GEMIT

IN ARIS IMMVNDIS
PYRAE ARDENT
DENSAE

PVNITOR
EARVM FLAMMAS HAVRIT

CANDIDIS IRAE OCVLIS

PHOEBEVS FVROR

Il cielo incandescente
Illumina
Il lento marmo delle acque

I cavalli del sole
Criniti di impetuosa violenza
Portano il furore di Apollo

Febea luce parte l'ombra

Il Dio sterminatore
L'Oscuro
Partorito da Latona bella chioma

Irato in cuore
Con l'arco d'argento
In fremito di dardi

Fa strage

Per nove giorni
Sul campo di papaveri cremisi

Quale letto di sangue danaide
Sotto ai piedi la terra geme cupa

Fra immondi altari
Le pire ardono
Fitte

Il Punitore
Ne beve le fiamme

In occhi candidi d'ira

Furore febeo

PHOEBVS (detail)
Brushed Steel and Cast Crystal (17"x10"x10" · 43x25x25cm)

PHOEBVS (detail)
Brushed Steel and Cast Crystal (17"x10"x10" · 43x25x25cm)

LACEDAEMONIVS OCCASVS

Hyacinth
By Zephyr violated in sepulchral silence

At vesper
On the occidental lands of Lacedaemon

Under the tears of Phoebus
Your visage
Covered by Tyrian purple
Indicates distances

Disarranged the hair
A veil of obscurity covers the eyes

Lowers the moist eyelids
Pure essence of pain

As an impure temple of melancholy
Your sepulchre in autumn
On the hills of Laconia

Becomes eternal symbol of loss
And continuous rebirth

Of Apollonian love

Occidental lands of Lacedaemon

HYACINTHE
A ZEPHYRO IN SILENTIO SEPVLCHRALI VIOLATE

VESPERI
IN OCCASV LACEDAEMONIO

SVB DACRVMIS PHOEBI
VVLTVS TVVS
PVRPVRA TYRIA SPARSVS
LONGINQVITATES INDICAT

TVRBATIS CAPILLIS
VELVM OBSCVRITATIS SVPER OCVLOS SE EXTENDIT

VDAS PALPEBRAS DEMITTIT
PVRA VIS DOLORIS

VT IMMORTALIS AEDES MAESTITIAE
SEPVLCHRVM TVVM AVTVMNO
IN COLLIBVS LACONIAE

FIT PERPETVVM SIGNVM AMISSIONIS
ET AD VITAM CONTINVI REDITVS

AMORIS APOLLINEI

LACEDAEMONIVS OCCASVS

Giacinto
Da Zefiro violato in sepolcrale silenzio

Al vespero
Sul ponente lacedemone

Sotto le lacrime di Febo
Il tuo volto
Coperto di porpora tiria
Indica lontananze

Sconvolti i capelli
Un velo di oscurita' si stende sugli occhi

Abbassa le umide palpebre
Pura essenza del dolore

Quale imperituro tempio della mestizia
Il tuo sepolcro in autunno
Sulle colline di Laconia

Diviene eterno simbolo della perdita
E continua rinascita

Dell' amore apollineo

Ponente lacedemone

THALAMOS

In the thalamus
Adorned with flowers of myrtle

You observe me
With your stare burnt of amber
Of the inebriated eyes

The body
Wrapped by most precious Assyrian silk
Of seduction woven

Sensitive hands
Caress buds of roses
Turgid

Tumid lips
Descend to the sweetest inguen
Of the taste of honey

In convulsion of pleasure
I taste its unquiet secretion
Copious

I assume its scent of violet cassis

The fire of an unrestrained desire
Slowly burns the marrow

Whilst furious caresses
Reverse the head

I pray you
My beloved
In correspondence of sensations

Breathe me to life

Thalamus

IN THALAMO
CANDIDIS FLORIBVS MYRTHI ORNATO

ELECTRO VSTV ADSPECTV
FLAGRANTIBVS OCVLIS
ME INTVERIS

CORPVS
SVBTILISSIMA BOMBYCE ASSYRIA INVOLVTVM
ILLECEBRAE INTEXTA

MOLLES MANVS
LEVITER ROSAS IN CALYCVLIS ADTINGVNT
TVRGIDIS

LABRA TVMIDA
DVLCISSIMA IN INGVINA DESCENDVNT
SVAVIA SAPORIS MELLIS

IN CONVVLSIONE VOLVPTATIS
GVSTO EORVM INQVIETVM LIQVOREM
COPIOSVM

ADSVMO EIVS EFFLVVIVM CYNOSBATI VIOLACEAE

ARDOR TEMERARIAE CVPIDITATIS
SENSIM MEDVLLAM FLAGRAT

DVM FVRENTES BLANDITIAE
CAPVT VERTVNT

TE ORO
MEA AMANS
IN CONVENIENTIA SENSVVM

ME IN VITAM RESPIRA

THALAMOS

Nel talamo
Adorno di candidi fiori di mirto

Mi osservi
Con il tuo sguardo bruciato d'ambra
Dagli occhi ebbri

Il corpo
Avvolto da preziosissima seta assiria
Intessuta di seduzione

Mani sensitive
Sfiorano rose in bocciolo
Turgido

Labbra tumide
Scendono all'inguine dolcissimo
Sapido di miele

In convulsione di volutta'
Ne assaporo la secrezione inquieta
Copiosa

Ne assumo l'effluvio di cassis violato

Il fuoco di un desiderio incontrollato
Arde lentamente il midollo

Mentre carezze furenti
Riversano il capo

Ti prego
Amante mia
In corrispondenza di sensazioni

Respirami in vita

Talamo

BEROLINVM

Night
A black and white photograph

A sudden light
Opens the perspective of the image

Obscure senses
Foreign
Wander on the damp cobblestone
Of the hyaline appearance

A c r i d   C o n t r a s t

People with no name
Dwell
In cramped urban theatres

Moist sombre shadows
Of elegant shape

And of sour smile

*Berlin
(Lichtenberg, MCMXCI)*

NOCTE
IMAGO ALBA ATRAQVE LVCE EXPRESSA

SVBITVM LVMEN
EIVS PROSPECTVM APERIT

OBSCVRI SENSVS
EXTRANEI
VDAM IN VIAM SILICEAM ERRANT
VITREO ASPECTV

A C R I S   D I S C R E P A N T I A

HOMINES SINE NOMINE
ANGVSTA THEATRA VRBANA
INCOLVNT

RORIDAE VMBRAE ATRAE
ELEGANTI FORMA

LENI AMARO RISV

BEROLINVM
(Lichtenberg, MCMXCI)

Notte
Una fotografia in bianco e nero

Una luce subitanea
Apre la prospettiva dell'immagine

Oscuri sensi
Estranei
Errano sul selciato umido
Dall'aspetto ialino

A c r e   C o n t r a s t o

Persone senza nome
Dimorano
In angusti teatri urbani

Roride ombre atre
Di elegante forma

E di amaro sorriso

Berlino
(Lichtenberg, MCMXCI)

EXCELSA CORRVPTIO

Our rage as lovers
In silence of innocence
Generates a premeditated violence

Irrational fear
Insane desire of pedication

The skin is lacerated
By outrageous tumidity

The body as instrument of domination

Because of me
On obscene soil
You suffer

You hold me
Between arrogance and inebriety
Contraction and spasm

T r a n s c e n d e n t   C o r r u p t i o n

As I
Draped with a residue of mud and rust
Reemerge
Among corrupt miasmas

Until bled dry
The wings close

In sublime breath

Transcendent corruption

NOSTRI AMANTIVM FVROR
IN SILENTIO CASTITATIS
MEDITATAM VIM GIGNIT

STVLTVM PAVOREM
CVPIDITATEM INSANAM PAEDICANDI

IMMVNDO TVMORE
CVTIS LACERATVR

CORPVS VT INSTRVMENTVM IMPERII

OB ME
IN OBSCENA TERRA
EXCRVCIARIS

ME AMPLECTERIS
INTER ADROGANTIAM ET EBRIETATEM
CONTRACTIO SPASMVSQVE

E X C E L S A C O R R V P T I O

ET EGO
MENSTRVIS EX LVTO ET ROBIGINE ORNATVS
DENVO EMERGO
IN INSALVBRIBVS MEPHITIBVS

DVM EXSANGVES
ALAE CLAVDVNT

PRECLARO ADFLATV

EXCELSA CORRVPTIO

La rabbia di noi amanti
In silenzio di innocenza
Genera una violenza premeditata

Irrazionale pavore
Desiderio insano di pedicazione

La pelle si lacera
Di un turgore immondo

Il corpo quale strumento di imperio

A causa mia
Su una terra oscena
Soffri

Mi stringi
Fra arroganza ed ebbrezza
Contrazione e spasimo

E m p i r e a   C o r r u z i o n e

Ed io
Drappeggiato da un mestruo di fango e ruggine
Riemergo
Fra malsani miasmi

Finche' dissanguate
Le ali si chiudono

In sublime afflato

Corruzione empirea

LENIS TREMOR

I come close to you in the bed of Tarquinia
With unquiet hands I caress your virginal skin

I perceive her subtle tremble sublime

Subtle tremble

TIBI IN TARQVINIENSI LECTO ADPROPINQVO
VIRGINALEM CVTIM TVAM
INQVIETIS MANIBVS PERMVLCEO

ANIMADVERTO EIVS LENEM MIRVM TREMOREM

LENIS TREMOR

Mi accosto a te nel letto di Tarquinia
Con mani inquiete accarezzo la tua pelle virginale

Ne avverto il lene fremore empireo

Lene fremore

IRIS VIRIDIS

You suddenly appear
As you walk away with a delicate step
Adorably laughing with your companions of games

The hair of amber
Gathered on the neck
Emerge to the sight
Filtered by an inclining sun on a translucent horizon

I approach you
Noble sister of Elyssa
I gently caress your back

You turn

For an instant
You stare at me
With your iris of green

The stillness of the gaze
Among the shadows of the lovable eyelashes
Dilates the flowing of time

Your visage of bronze

The superb cheeks between the circular pendants
The neck adorned with purest pearls

Your slender body wrapped in Bactrian silk
In a diffused scent of late roses
Of perfumed dresses

The space becomes vacuous
Pure
Your companions vanish in the Phoebic light

I am
Finally alone
Before you

Opened the feminine smile
With subdued voice
You lovably say my name
As only my father could do

Without words
With a slow gesture
I dare to draw my lips close to yours of the sweetest moistness

Adorned with dew
Ooze virginal honey

A subtle tremble shakes me

You wrap your arms around me
With sensitive hands
You welcome me within your fervid embrace

Drinking at your sisterly soul

I am born again

Green iris

MIHI IMPROVISO APPARES
DVM LEVI GRADV ABIS
TVIS CVM COMITIBVS LVDORVM DVLCE RIDENS

CAPILLVS SVCINVS
IN CERVICE SVBTILI COLLIGATVS
VISVI PATEFACIT
SOLE IN PERLVCIDO CAELO INCLINANTI EFFLVXVS

TE CONSEQVOR
NOBILIS SOROR ELISSAE
LEVITER TERGVM TVVM ADTINGO

TE VERTIS

MOMENTVM TEMPORIS
ME INTVERIS
IRIDE TVA VIRIDI

IMMOBILITAS ASPECTVS
IN AMABILIVM CILIIORVM VMBRA
TEMPVS DILATAT FLVENS

VVLTVS TVVS AENEVS

GENAE SINVATAS INTER INAVRES SPLENDIDAE
COLLVM MARGERITIIS PVRISSIMIS ORNATVM

CORPVS TVVS SVBTILIS BOMBYCE BACTRIAE AMICTVS
IN ODORE ROSARVM SERARVM EFFVSO
VESTIS FRAGRANTIS

SPATIVM VACVVM FIT
PVRVM
COMITES TVAE EVANESCVNT IN PHOEBEIA LVCE

SVM
AD VLTIMVM SOLVS
IN TVI COSPECTV

FEMINEO RISV APERTO
VOCE SVBMISSA
MEVM NOMEN AMABILITER DICIS
QVEM AD MODVM MEVS PATER SOLVM FACERE SCIEBAT

SINE VERBIS
GESTV LENTO
MEA LABRA AVDEO ADMOVERE TVIS HVMORE
DOLCISSIMO

RORE ORNATIS
MELLA MANANT VIRGINALIA

SVBTILIS TREMOR ME COMMOVET

TVIS BRACHIIS ME CINGIS
MANIBVS SENSIBILIBVS
ME ACCIPIS IN COMPLEXVM TVVM FERVIDVM

EX TVA ANIMA BIBENS SOROR

RENASCOR

IRIS VIRIDIS

A me imprevisto appari
Mentre ti allontani con passo leggiero
Ridendo dolcemente con le tue compagne di giuoco

I capelli di ambra
Raccolti sulla nuca sottile
Affiorano alla vista
Filtrati da un sole inclinantesi su un orizzonte diafano

Ti raggiungo
Nobile sorella di Elissa
Lievemente ti sfioro la schiena

Ti volgi

Per un istante
Mi fissi
Con la tua iride viridea

L'immobilita' dello sguardo
Fra l'ombra delle ciglia amabili
Dilata lo scorrere del tempo

Il tuo volto eneo

Le guance superbe fra i pendenti circolari
Il collo adornato di perle purissime

Il tuo corpo sottile avvolto da seta di Bactria
In odore effuso di rose tarde
Di aulenti vesti

Lo spazio diviene vacuo
Puro
Le tue compagne vaniscono nella luce febica

Sono
Finalmente solo
Di fronte a te

Dischiuso il sorriso femmineo
Con voce sommessa
Pronunci amabilmente il mio nome
Come solo mio padre sapeva fare

Senza parole
Con gesto lento
Oso accostare le mie labbra alle tue dall'umidore dolcissimo

Imperlate di rugiada
Stillano miele vergine

Un tremore sottile mi scuote

Mi cingi con le tue braccia
Con mani sensitive
Mi accogli entro il tuo abbraccio fervido

Bevendo dalla tua sororea anima

Rinasco

Iride viridea

EBRIETAS

The sea breathes
Pants in lucid delirium

Inconstant

Under the promontories sacred to the olive tree

The acridness of waters
Diffuses
A marine scent
Of acerbic citruses

As

My purest individualism
Shivers
Of intimate anguish
Of sudden inquietudes

Insane tremble

And violent impulse

Inebriety

MARE SPIRAT
IN LVCIDO DELIRIO ANHELAT

MVTABILE

SVB PROMVNTVRIIS OLEAE SACRIS

ACRIMONIA AQVARVM
EFFVNDIT
ODOREM AEQVOREVM
ACERBORVM ACRIVM POMORVM

VT

AMOR MEI PVRISSIMVS
TREMIT
INTIMA SOLLICITVDINE
CVRIS SVBITIS

TREPIDATIO INSANA

ET VIOLENTA IMPVLSIO

EBRIETAS

Il mare respira
In lucido delirio ansima

Mutevole

Sotto promontori sacri all'olivo

L'acredine delle acque
Effonde
Un odore equoreo
Di aspri agrumi

Come

Il mio individualismo purissimo
Trema
Di intimo travaglio
Di inquietudini subitanee

Insano fremito

E violenta pulsione

Ebrieta'

RESCVSATIO

Free in time
Lover in action
Flowers hands dew and kisses

Pause

Then rain and sighs
A light breathing
The intense action

Imperfection of the being who lives amongst experience love and most
of all freedom

Mechanical gestures
Breaths and impulses
As far as here, until now
Sudden rebounds of things bound to fall

Reaction

Impulses and breaths
Instinctively I tremble

Reaction

Poetic translation by Marco Mathieu of "I breathe"
from SITIS PERPETVA by Stefano Losi

*"Each of the two of us was writing verses, in this or the other meter,
taking turns…"*

LIBER IN TEMPORE
AGENS AMATOR
FLORES MANVS ROS ET BASIA

MORA

DEINDE IMBER ET SVSPIRIA
TENVIS ANIMA
ACTIO VEHEMENS

VITIVM ANIMANTIS QVI INTER VSVS AMOREM ET
PRAESERTIM LIBERTATEM VIVIT

MECHANICI GESTVS
SPIRITVS ET IMPVLSIONES
ADHVC, VSQVE AD HOC TEMPVS
SVBITI SALTVS CASVRARVM RERVM

RESCVSATIO

IMPVLSIONES ET SPIRITVS
SPONTE TREMO

RESCVSATIO

"SCRIBENS VERSICVLOS VTERQVE NOSTRVM
LVDEBAT NVMERO MODO HOC MODO ILLOC

REDDENS MVTVA PER IOCVM ATQVE VINVM
..."

Libero nel tempo
Amante in azione
Fiori mani rugiada e baci

Pausa

Poi pioggia e sospiri
Un respiro leggero
L'azione intensa

Imperfezione dell'essere che vive tra esperienze amore e soprattutto
liberta'

Gesti meccanici
Respiri e pulsioni
Fino a qui, fino ad ora
Rimbalzi improvvisi di cose destinate a cadere

Reazione

Pulsioni e respiri
Istintivamente tremo

Reazione

Traduzione poetica di Marco Mathieu di "Respiro"
da SITIS PERPETVA di Stefano Losi

"Ognuno di noi due scriveva versi in questo o quell'altro metro, a turno…"

"[...] AT NON EFFVGIES MEOS IAMBOS"